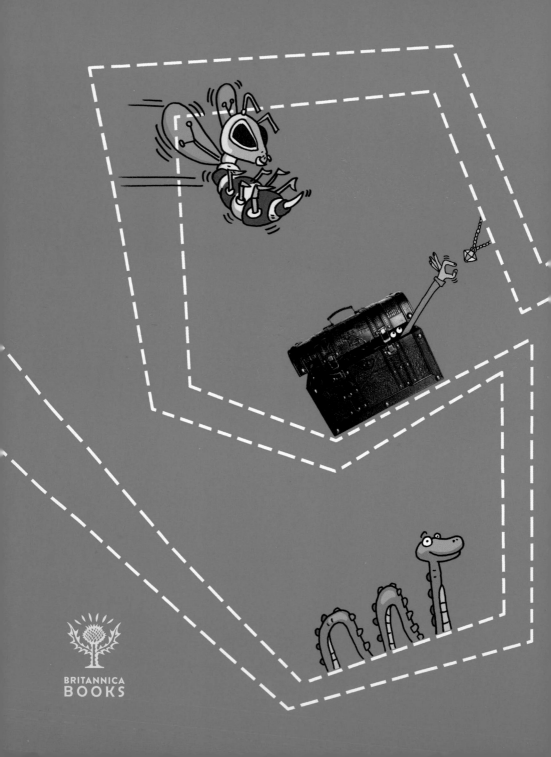

SECRET

FACTopia!

Follow the TRAIL of 400 HIDDEN FACTS

By PAIGE TOWLER

Illustrated by ANDY SMITH

CONTENTS

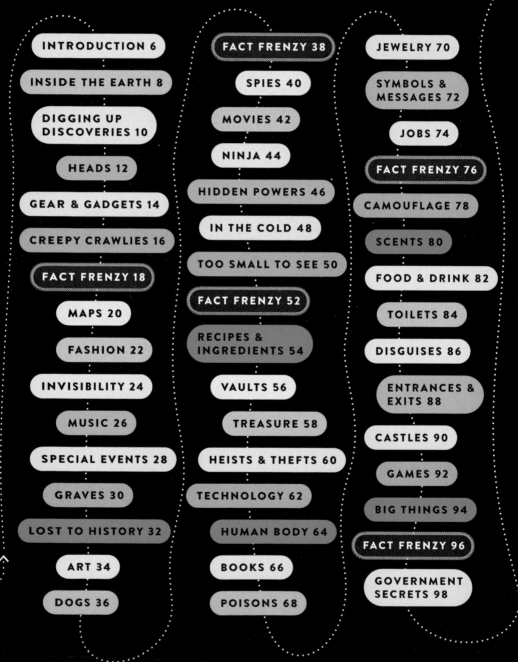

Explore the secretive side of FACTopia!

Get ready for a fun-filled undercover journey through little-known facts about disguises, invisibility, the world beneath your feet, and more.

This clandestine adventure takes you through hundreds of the most mind-blowing, wow-worthy, and crazy-cool classified facts. For example...

Did you know that bloodhounds can follow invisible scent trails for 130 miles (209km)?

Speaking of invisible things, a Japanese engineer has developed a real-life invisibility cloak that uses tiny light-reflecting beads to hide its wearer.

But that's not the only amazing technology you'll find—or maybe you won't! The ancient Byzantines supposedly created ships that could shoot a fiery substance—but the recipe has since disappeared.

And if you want more history:
For centuries, people across eastern
Asia have used crickets to help detect
unseen intruders in their homes.

You might have spotted that there is something special about being here in FACTopia. Every fact is linked to the next, and in the most surprising and even hilarious ways.

On this mysterious FACTopia tour, you will encounter top secrets*, unsolved mysteries, dark caves, deep ocean dwellers, hidden history, and ... well, you'll see. Discover what each turn of the page will bring!

But there isn't just one trail through this book. Your path branches every now and then, and you can zip forward and backward to go to a totally different (but still connected) part of FACTopia.

Let your curiosity take you wherever it leads. Of course, a good place to start could be right here, at the beginning.

*The facts are not the only secrets in this book. Hidden among the pages you can find ten mice, like the one here, which are concealed in unexpected places. So grab your magnifying glass, put on your detective gear, and see if you can spot them all!

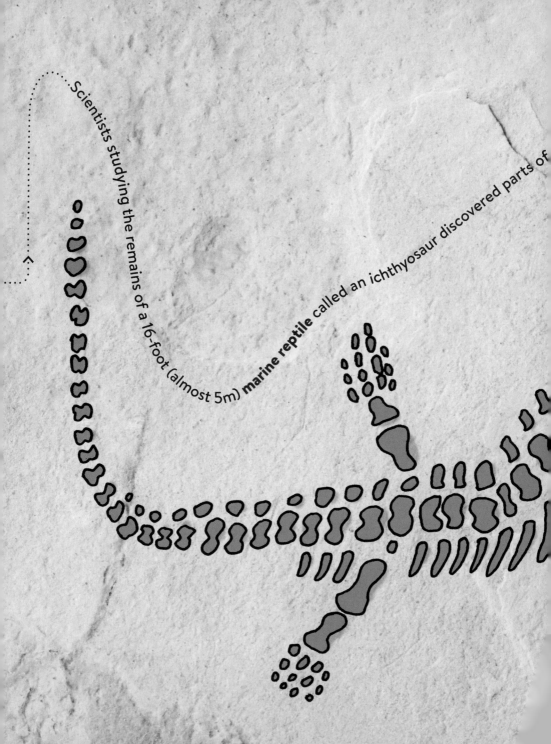

Scientists studying the remains of a 16-foot (almost 5m) **marine reptile** called an ichthyosaur discovered parts of

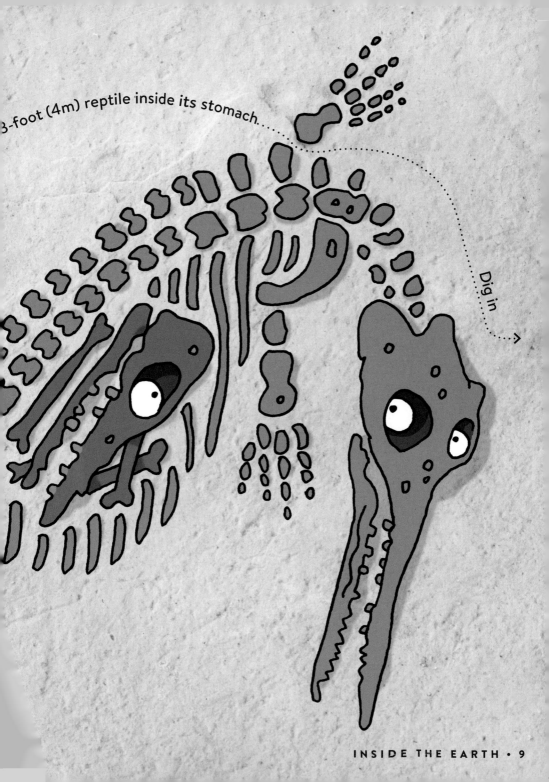

...-foot (4m) reptile inside its stomach....

Dig in →

THE DEEPEST HOLE EVER DRILLED BY HUMANS IS IN RUSSIA AND DESCENDS SO FAR DOWNWARD THAT THE TALLEST BUILDING ON EARTH COULD FIT INSIDE NEARLY 15 TIMES

Paleontologists in China discovered a **fossilized dinosaur egg**—inside was a fossilized baby dinosaur that had been preparing to hatch.

The **Tully Monster** fossil was dug up from an Illinois coal mine in the 1950s. It is so strange that most information about the animal—such as whether or not it had a backbone—is still a mystery, and scientists can only guess at what the monster looked like.

Scientists searching the desert in Egypt have discovered the fossil of a 1,323-pound (600kg), **four-legged whale** that lived both on land and in water about 43 million years ago.

Heads up

A **140,000-year-old skull** found in China is known as the Dragon Man and may belong to a previously undiscovered species of human.

Cockroaches have one brain inside their heads, and a series of nerve clusters in their abdomens that function as a **"second brain"**

In the 1990s, a statue's head was **stolen from a cemetery** in Canada—only to be mysteriously returned some 20 years later.

Known as the "Easter Island Heads," the moai—giant statues carved by the Rapa Nui people on an island off Chile—also have **enormous bodies** that have sunk into the ground

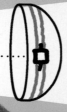

One company has invented a **contact lens** that can record video and take pictures.

All the gear

There are more than *six billion bacteria* in the average adult's mouth.

Bold bacteria

Go to page 173

During the Cold War, Soviet spies in what is now Russia sometimes wore **rings that could take photographs**—but each ring could snap only one picture...

Just jewelry

People today can buy **security cameras** disguised to look like teddy bears, smoke detectors, toilet brushes, and more...

Go to page 70

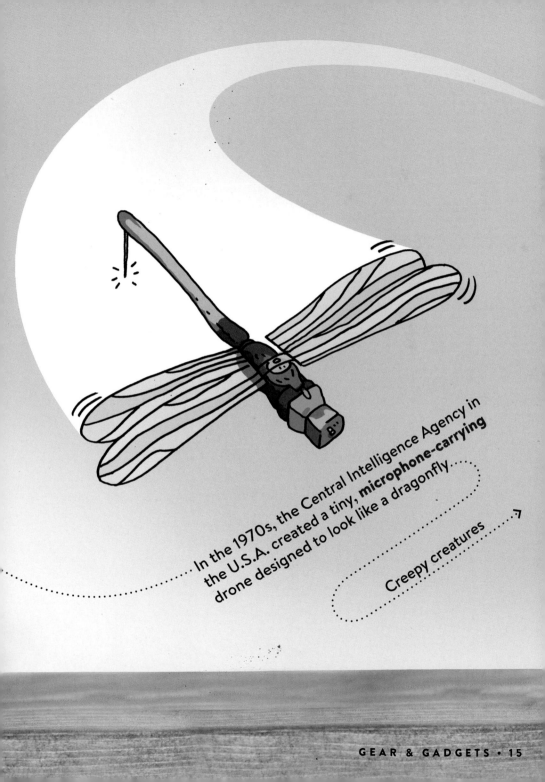

In the 1970s, the Central Intelligence Agency in the U.S.A. created a tiny, **microphone-carrying** drone designed to look like a dragonfly.

Creepy creatures

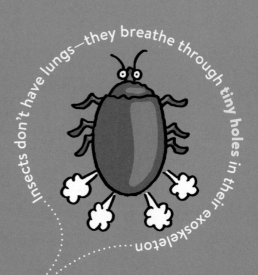

Insects don't have lungs—they breathe through tiny holes in their exoskeleton

The **giant burrowing cockroach**—the only cockroach known to live and hide in permanent burrows—is about the size of an adult's palm and can dig up to 3 feet (1m) underground

Locals in Thailand discovered a **"hairy" snake**. Scientists think that the "fur" may be algae that grew while the snake waited patiently for prey

Deep in the Waitomo Caves in New Zealand, some glowworms use water and their own urine to create a glowing, sticky substance that traps prey.

Catch a spider

Some species of spiders hunt in packs by communicating to each other through invisible vibrations in their webs.

Creepy caves

Go to page 134

Located in China, the imperial **palace** known as the Forbidden City was off-limits to everyone except the emperor and his guests for nearly six centuries.

A 100-million-year-old spider became trapped in a piece of amber as it attacked its prey—creating the only known **fossil** of its kind.

The first ever **fossil** of a sleeping dinosaur was uncovered in China.

Visitors can see artifacts that are mostly invisible to the naked eye at a **museum** in Washington, D.C., by scanning them with special devices.

One **museum** in Puebla, Mexico, is located in a system of 500-year-old underground tunnels.

In 1901, Russian artisans carved a tiny **palace** of gold and placed it inside a priceless Fabergé egg.

To keep their eggs safe, some species of **fish** carry them in their mouths in a process called mouthbrooding.

When it is young, one species of **fish**, called the surgeonfish, is transparent and partly invisible.

The world's longest and deepest train tunnel took 17 years to build and runs more than 1.4 miles (2.3km) below the **mountains** in Switzerland.

The source of the Nile River was once thought by some to come from waters hidden within a mythical **mountain** range called the "Mountains of the Moon," which appeared on maps even though they didn't exist!

Map it out

Since the 1950s, government mapmakers in Switzerland have hidden **tiny drawings**—such as of animals and people—in official topographic maps.

One company in the U.K. turns escape maps, created for soldiers in World War II, into clothing.

Follow the trends →

Some companies make underwear with **secret pockets** that can be used to hide valuables..........

Many historic nomadic peoples in the Middle East **sewed coins** into items of clothing for decoration or safekeeping....

For centuries, women in Suriname have worn **headscarves** called *angisa* that can be folded in many different ways to communicate secret messages.

Go to page 110

More transportation

During the late 19th century in Europe and the U.S.A., it was considered inappropriate for women to wear pants—but it was unsafe for women to ride bicycles in long skirts. As a result, American designers created **"trouser skirts"**—pants attached and hidden under a skirt ...

...A Japanese engineer has developed a real-life **invisibility cloak** that uses tiny light-reflecting beads to hide its wearer.

Can you see it?

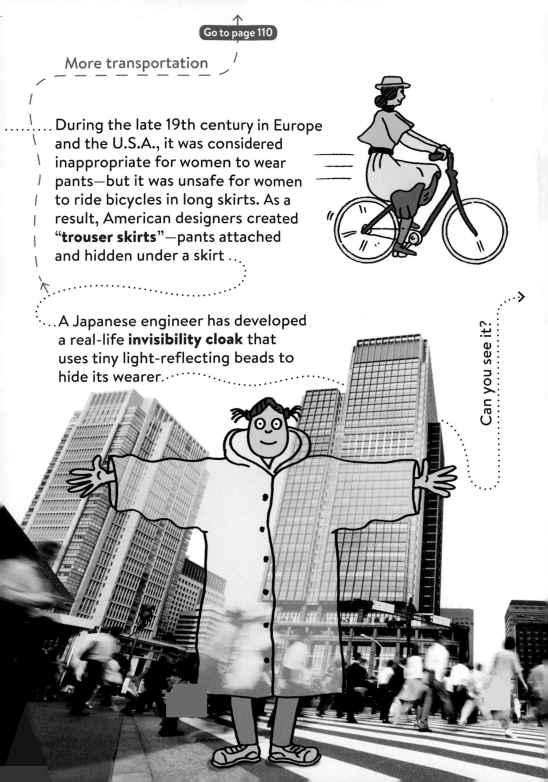

The **glasswing butterfly** has transparent wings

In a study, scientists used **virtual reality headsets** to convince participants that they had become

INVISIBLE

One house in the desert of California looks nearly invisible because it is made almost entirely of mirrors

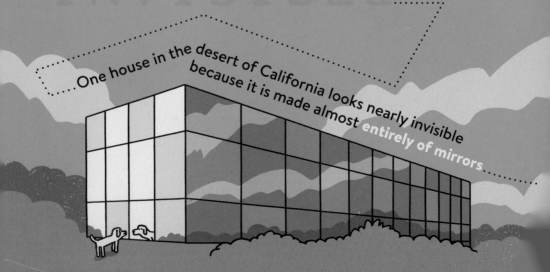

During the **Air Guitar World Championships** in Finland, contestants rock out on instruments that don't actually exist....

Music mayhem

One Swiss-born philosopher's attempt to make invisible ink went horribly wrong when the **concoction exploded** in his face....

Go to page 116

"**Backmasking**" is when a singer records a message backward on to a song that is playing forward. The listener can hear the secret message only by playing the song in reverse.

Stradivarius violins make a **unique sound** among violins. Experts think it is the result of Stradivari, the 17th–18th-century violin-maker, soaking the instruments' wood in a secret mix of chemicals.

One university orchestra holds concerts inside the world's **oldest-known cave system**, formed some 240 million years ago in what is now South Africa

You're invited

...⟩......One **cemetery** in New York has a grave for secrets. Visitors whisper their confessions to the tombstone or write them down on slips of paper, then put them into a hole in the stone..................

Feeling lost?

According to legend, famed Mongol leader Genghis Khan asked to be **buried in secret**. His followers hid the location so well that, to this day, no one can find it

Go to page 66

In the books

For hundreds (perhaps thousands) of years, women in parts of China communicated between themselves using a **secret language** called Nüshu.

...In the 7th century, the Byzantines of what is now Turkey invented ship

In the 16th century, artists in parts of Europe created **cobweb art**, a form of painting that used the transparent silk produced by spiders, moths, and caterpillars as canvasses. Fewer than 100 of these paintings survive today.

Amazing art >

at could spew a flaming substance called

GREEK FIRE

—to this day, no one knows how they made it.

Go to page 166

To robots

Scientists trained technology to use satellites to find previously undiscovered ancient works of art in Peru

artificial intelligence

One archaeobotanist searches Renaissance paintings for images of fruit to learn about plants that may have become extinct

Hidden compartments in a 700-year-old Buddhist statue contained some 150 historical artifacts, such as scrolls, figurines, and other relics

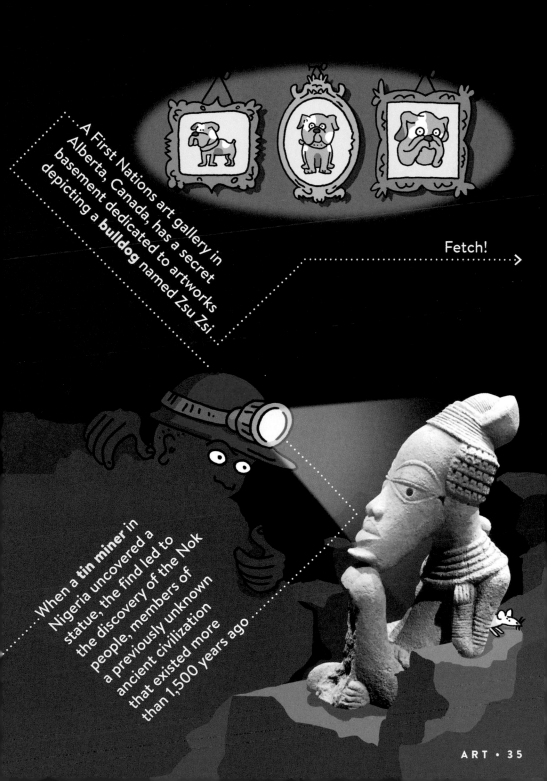

A First Nations art gallery in Alberta, Canada, has a secret basement dedicated to artworks depicting a **bulldog** named Zsu Zsi.

Fetch!

When a **tin miner** in Nigeria uncovered a statue, the find led to the discovery of the Nok people, members of a previously unknown ancient civilization that existed more than 1,500 years ago

Bloodhounds can follow **invisible** scent trails for som

.....The Komondor, a Hungarian breed of dog with

ropelike white fur,

was bred to blend in with sheep to better protect them....

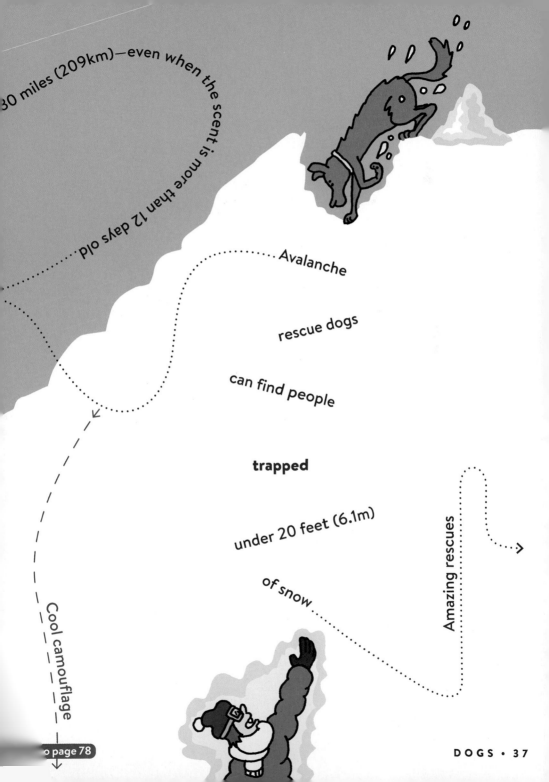

30 miles (209km)—even when the scent is more than 12 days old

Avalanche

rescue dogs

can find people

trapped

under 20 feet (6.1m)

of snow

Amazing rescues

Cool camouflage

o page 78

If an object vanishes in your home and then reappears again, it is known as the "**disappearing object phenomenon**."

Disappearing sculptures made by one German artist look solid from most angles but seem to completely vanish from others.

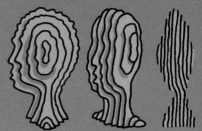

Some artists use **nut** shells to craft small boxes for hiding jewelry.

Designed to look like a pile of **logs**, one home in the Netherlands is nearly completely camouflaged in the woods.

One Italian artist carves "pop-up" wooden castles into **logs**. The castles can pop up out of the wood or collapse back into it.

During World War II, a Chinese soldier was lost on a raft in the **ocean** for 133 days—and survived.

Using technology based on a squid's ability to camouflage itself, scientists are devising stickers that could make objects **invisible**.

Sperm whales can dive deep into the **ocean** where it is almost completely dark to hunt giant squid.

So many **nuts** are hidden by squirrels during the fall that the squirrels often forget where they've buried them.

Police in Iran once arrested a group of squirrels that they believed to be spies.

Go undercover

People lost in the world's largest corn **maze** in Dixon, California, have been known to call the police for help.

Samurai would hide in concealed rooms within a **maze** of passages inside Japan's Himeji Castle.

In a Haudenosaunee **legend**, corn husk dolls are faceless because a Corn Spirit hid a doll's face when the doll grew too vain.

Invisible to the human eye, there are at least 1,000 different species of fungi known as microfungi.

Fungi that grow in a circle are often called fairy rings. They are depicted in **legends** as being made by fairies, elves, or spirits.

During the American Civil War, a formerly enslaved woman named Mary Jane Richards served as a spy and **successfully infiltrated** the Confederate Senate to learn about its war plans

Saraswathi Rajamani, India's first-known **female** spy, began working to obtain information for Indian independence when she was just 16

During World War II, Juan Pujol García, from Spain, acted as a **double agent**—he pretended to spy for the Nazis but actually passed information to the Allies. He faked his own death—and kept it secret for 36 years

That's classified!

Go to page 98

"007," the code name for **James Bond**, a fictional British spy in books and movies, was first used by a 16th-century spy for Britain's Queen Elizabeth I, who supposedly signed his secret letters using those numbers........

Action!

According to some scholars, spies in

ancient Egypt

were known as the "Eyes of the Pharaoh"......

The Academy Awards, a yearly film awards ceremony held in **Hollywood**, California, are so secretive that only two people are allowed to count the ballots to find out who wins

To make the sound of a *Tyrannosaurus rex* roaring in the Jurassic Park movies, **sound engineers** used tiger snarls, alligator gurgles, and baby elephant squeals. The sound of the dinosaur's breathing was a whale sending air out of its blowhole

Strange jobs

Go to page

The way of ninja

In many ninja or kung-fu movies featuring **near-impossible stunts**, actors rely on a technique known as "wire fu": being hoisted by wires so thin as to be invisible or later digitally removed

Ninja—also called *shinobi*—were spies who practiced a mix of **espionage and martial arts** known as ninjutsu.

Female ninja were known as kunoichi, and sometimes used a weapon called a neko-te, or "cat hand": a claw designed to look like a cat's paw.

Ninja may have avoided STRONG-SMELLING FOODS or eaten vegetarian diets to help get rid of body odor and avoid detection.

Because ninja were both well trained and mysterious, people sometimes thought they had **superpowers** such as flight, invisibility, or the ability to walk on water.

Pee-yew!

Go to page 80

Ninja sometimes used *shuriken*—sharp, **star-shape weapons** that could be thrown to distract enemies.

Hidden superpowers

Go to page 82

Delicious!

Catfish have so many **tastebuds** that they can hunt without eyesight, relying just on their sense of taste to find food.

Some people can train themselves to

echolocate

—to sense where nearby objects are by making a clicking noise and listening for the sound vibrations that bounce back.

Jewel beetles can sense fire from about 50 miles (80km) away.

Some birds glow under **ULTRAVIOLET LIGHT**

Some people have a **gene** that makes them less affected by the cold.

Brrr!

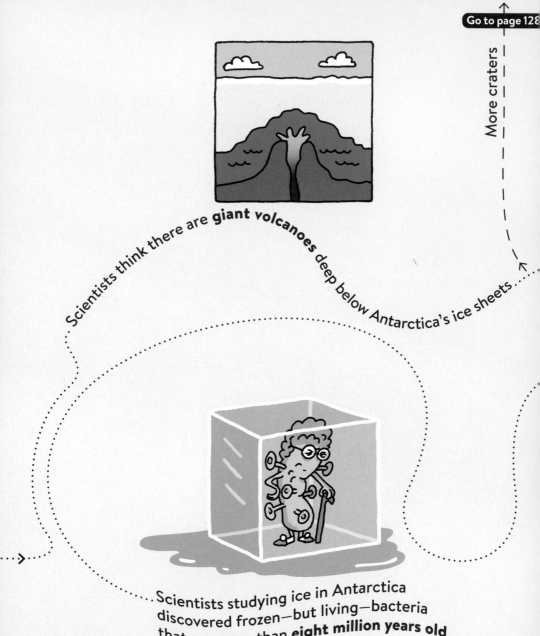

Go to page 128

More craters

Scientists think there are **giant volcanoes** deep below Antarctica's ice sheets...

Scientists studying ice in Antarctica discovered frozen—but living—bacteria that are more than **eight million years old**...

Japanese scientists discovered a chemical in strawberries that can be used to create ice cream that doesn't MELT

Teeny tiny.

In one competition in France, scientists built tiny, **microscopic cars made of only** molecules—and then raced them...

One
British
artist
makes
sculptures
so
small
they
can
fit
inside
the
eye
of
a
needle
and
need
a
microscope
to
be
seen...

Super sculptures

————————>

Teenagers helping an archaeological dig in Israel discovered a hoard of pure **gold** coins that had been hidden in a **pot** more than 1,100 years ago.

Some historians think the piggy bank originated more than 600 years ago, when people in parts of Indonesia stashed their loose coins in metal or clay **pots** shaped like **pigs**!

Some insects—such as certain termites and **ants**—collect **gold** and store it in their nests.

One Indian scientist discovered that the **transparent** abdomen of one type of **ant** will change to the color of whatever food the ant has eaten.

The petals of the skeleton **flower** look white when they are dry but turn **transparent** when they get wet.

The **mind** of an orb weaver spider can be controlled by the ichneumonid **wasp**.

One Italian artist auctioned off an "invisible" sculpture. It doesn't actually exist— instead it is meant to be imagined in the **mind** of the person who buys it.

The fairy **wasp** is so **tiny** that a female can hide her eggs inside the eggs of other insects.

Researchers studying **pigs** developed an **artificial intelligence** that can analyze a pig's grunts to reveal if the pig's emotions are positive or negative.

Scientists created an **artificial intelligence** that can examine a photograph of a food dish, then reveal the ingredients and recipe needed to cook that dish.

Time to eat

Hungry for **pollen**, harvest mice sometimes crawl inside **flowers** and then fall asleep there.

Just one ragweed plant can contain **billons** of **pollen** grains that are invisible to the human eye.

Filopodia are microscopic, antennae-like **tentacles** that help your **cells** move around.

Tiny aquatic organisms invisible to the human eye, known as Bryozoa, use **tentacles** around their mouths to eat.

Scientists aren't sure how many **cells** are in the human body—estimates range from **billions** to millions of trillions.

Go to page 114

Awesome amusement parks

During the Covid-19 lockdowns, Disney released several recipes for its famed **theme-park snacks** so people could make the treats at home.

To make sriracha, a **spicy sauce** first made in Thailand, a chef designed machinery so unique that the sauce can't be re-created without it.

The recipe for **Coca-Cola** is so secret that it is kept locked in a vault

Lock it up ›

The Svalbard Global Seed Vault in Norway is carved more than 328 feet (100m) into a mountain and houses **MILLIONS OF SEED SAMPLES**

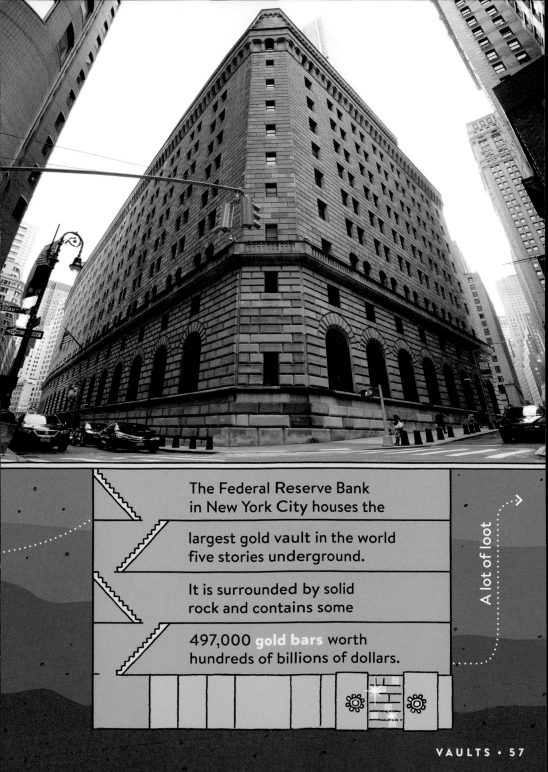

The Federal Reserve Bank in New York City houses the

largest gold vault in the world five stories underground.

It is surrounded by solid rock and contains some

497,000 **gold bars** worth hundreds of billions of dollars.

A lot of loot

Go to page 10

Dig it up

A couple walking their dog in California decided to investigate a discarded metal can—and discovered a hoard of century-old **gold coins** worth about $10 million......

..... A team of thieves managed to clear out **six display cases of jewels** worth millions of dollars from a museum in the Netherlands—without getting caught on security cameras—and authorities still have no idea how they did it.....

Stop, thief! ···>

....According to legend, an 18th-century woman in Liechtenstein committed several robberies by using a large trunk. At night, a hidden accomplice would **crawl out** of the trunk to steal nearby valuables...

...One group of thieves in Jamaica made an **entire beach** disappear by stealing all the sand...

In 1671, a man named Thomas Blood and his accomplices attempted to steal the **Crown Jewels** of England by flattening some pieces with a hammer, sawing others in half, and storing some down their pants.

According to folklore originating in the U.K., invisible fairies or witches often try to **steal butter** on a holiday known as May Day.

During World War II, German spies used a machine known as the **Enigma** to encode messages. To steal important information, British mathematician Alan Turing built an entirely new machine designed to crack the Enigma's codes.

Geek out

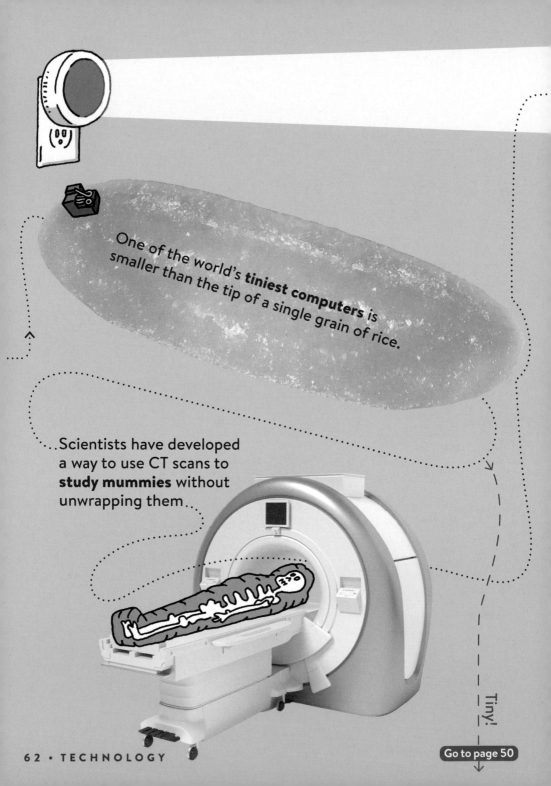

One of the world's **tiniest computers** is smaller than the tip of a single grain of rice.

Scientists have developed a way to use CT scans to **study mummies** without unwrapping them.

Tiny!

Go to page 50

Several companies are working to create a device that can charge phones with **invisible beams of energy** that restore the battery power through the air.

Inside your body

Scientists recently developed a computer program that may be able to solve the mystery of how **dinosaurs moved and walked**.

Experts are creating technology that can be **implanted into the skin or brain** that will let people interact with computers without touching them.

Platinum—one of the

MOST EXPENSIVE

natural metals—is found in tiny amounts in the human body.

During the European Renaissance, scientists often created and used **lift-the-flap books** to study human anatomy; each flap would lift up to reveal the body's inner workings.

Read all about it

The world's oldest-known printed, dated book—an 1,100-year-old copy of a Buddhist text called the *Diamond Sutra*—was sealed away in a cave in China.

ULTRAVIOLET LIGHT can reveal the writings in ancient books that have faded over the centuries.

Back in time

Go to page 32

One 17th-century German book contains
a **hollowed space** with a hidden stash of poisons.

That's toxic!

Nearly every single part of the manchineel tree, found in some tropical places in the Americas, is poisonous—it even contains **poisonous sap** inside it.

According to legend, an ancient Persian king came up with a **universal antidote**—a recipe that could cure any poison—but the recipe has since been lost.

Poison rings—which have existed for centuries—have a secret compartment to hold the deadly potion.

Dazzling

Archaeologists at an Inca site in Peru discovered a burial of some **100 guinea pigs** wearing earrings and necklaces.

One designer makes a bejeweled bracelet that looks like a snake but has a **secret watch** in a compartment in its mouth.

During the 18th century, rings were sometimes made with a hidden compartment underneath the gem that was filled with **scented powders**— so if things got too stinky, the wearer could sniff their ring instead.

Acrostic jewelry uses the first letter of each **gemstone** in the piece—"e" for emerald, and so on—to send a secret message....

Some companies make necklaces that can contain secret messages in **Morse code**.

L O V E

Get the message

For thousands of years, people have used

smoke signals—messages sent by building huge fires

and creating smoke patterns—to communicate

quickly or secretly over distances.

Used throughout Europe beginning around the 13th century, **letterlocking** is the practice of folding or cutting a letter so that it stays "locked" shut and its contents are kept secret

Go to page 82

Eat up

During World War I and World War II, U.S. postal workers were recruited to check for hidden enemy messages in the mail.

Hard at work

According to a Chinese folktale, a group once planned a successful rebellion against an invading ruler by sending messages to one another inside pastries known as **mooncakes**.

In Colombia, enslaved Afro-Colombian women communicated in secret by **braiding messages** into their hair.

...Before bowling lanes were fully automated, people called **pinsetters** worked unseen behind the lanes and machinery to re-set pins after they'd been knocked down...

In the Middle Ages, Venetian **GLASSBLOWERS** were required to move to the island of Murano to protect their secret methods—and they weren't allowed to leave!

Time to play

Go to page 92

Professional underwater golf-ball retrievers don wetsuits and **dive deep** into the ponds on golf courses to find lost balls......

More down there

Some shrimp are covered in bright, almost neon stripes that help them hide among the many **colors** of anemones and coral.

Some divers have had their **teeth** cleaned by tiny shrimp.

White rhinos can use the scents hidden in piles of **poop** to communicate with each other.

To **communicate** about their clans, status, and more, many ancient Jomon people, of what is now Japan, removed teeth to create gaps that gave the information.

A strange structure known as the Yonaguni Monument, submerged off the coast of Japan, may be the base of an ancient **pyramid**.

The **Pyramid** of the Moon, in Mexico, was built on top of a cave, which ancient Mesoamericans may have believed was an entrance to the underworld.

Scientists think that the orange **color** in a tiger's stripes may appear green to some prey.

Hidden in plain sight

Scientists found a newly discovered species of beetle in a 230-million-year-old piece of fossilized dinosaur **poop**.

Researchers are developing a new device that lets humans breathe **underwater**, inspired by diving beetles that surround themselves in bubbles of oxygen.

One cave in Czechia, known as the Hranice Abyss, is the deepest freshwater cave in the world, sinking more than 3,280 feet (1,000m) **underwater**.

By staying very still, tilting its head, and closing its eyes, the **tawny frogmouth bird** can make itself look just like a tree branch

Young masked hunter bugs have **sticky hairs** on their body to catch dust, sand, and other small particles so that they can blend into their surroundings

As its name suggests, the **leaf-tailed gecko** can disguise itself to look like leaves.

Some plants have evolved to look like **stones**, probably so that they don't get eaten.

The puff adder snake is so good at using "olfactory camouflage"—hiding by **disguising its scent**—that even dogs can't sniff it out.

Take a whiff

Peculiar plants

Go to page 108

A French perfume company studies **individual molecules** to create scents that can mimic the unique smell of any person.

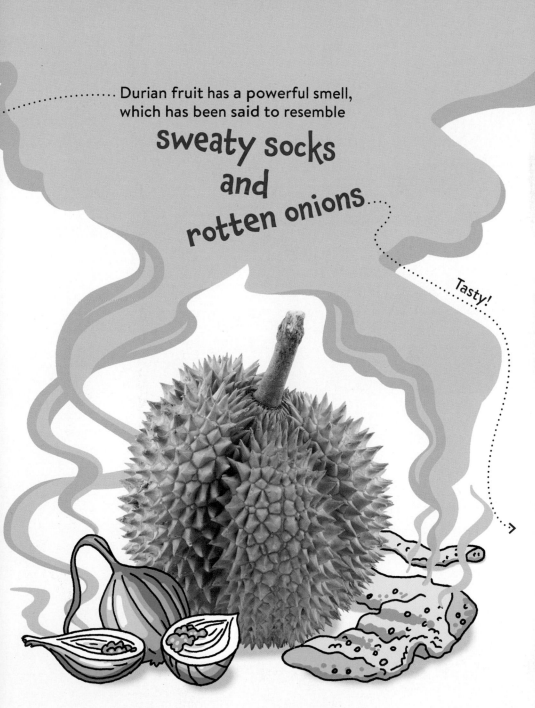

Durian fruit has a powerful smell, which has been said to resemble

sweaty socks and rotten onions

Tasty!

Probably originating in eastern Asia more than 4,000 years ago, tasseography is the art of using someone's **leftover tea leaves** to predict their future.

In the 19th century, farmers in France began using **underground quarries and tunnels** to grow mushrooms—including in the underground cemetery of bones known as the Catacombs.

Researchers in Denmark discovered **buried drink barrels** more than 300 years old, only to find out that they were full of ancient human poop.

Ew!

...According to legend, only two people on the planet officially know how to **fold a napkin** in a style called the Hapsburg fold, originally created in Austria...

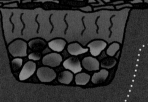

From Polynesia to South America to India, chefs still use an ancient barbecuing technique that involves **cooking foods** in a pit under the ground...

Head below

Go to page 104

Made in the 18th century, the toilet in one house in Belgium is disguis

o look like a stack of books

What is that?

Go to page 174

More rulers

In the early 2000s, King Abdullah II of Jordan took to **going undercover** to check on how the country was being run, variously disguising himself as an elderly man, a reporter, or a taxi driver.

The American CIA once created a **radio transmitter** disguised to look like a piece of dog poop.

Woof!

Go to page 36

Enslaved Africans forcibly transported to Brazil created the martial art capoeira, which they **disguised as a dance** so they could practice it without being discovered by their captors.

In the 1800s, a Brazilian woman named **Maria Quitéria** disguised herself as a man to join the army and fight for Brazilian independence.

The entrance to one clothing store in Boston, Massachusetts, is disguised to look like a **soda machine**.

Enter here →

The entrance to one **secret beach** in Indonesia is down the side of a steep cliff shaped like a *Tyrannosaurus rex*...

Archaeologists discovered a hidden door in Scotland's 18th-century Culzean Castle that leads to a system of caves below

Storm the castle

In the 1950s in England, a secret 35-acre (14.2ha) **underground city** called Burlington was built to house up to 4,000 government workers. It had hidden entrances at ground level.

The jungle completely covered an **Australian castle** after it was abandoned in the 1930s—and it was rediscovered only sixty years later.

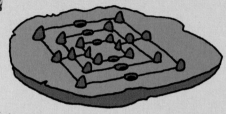

Historians working in a medieval castle in Russia discovered a room that contained a board game similar to an **early version of checkers.**

Let's play! ›

The largest-ever game of **hide-and-seek** took place in China and involved 1,437 people.

海窩水暖且將龍引來

戊戌夏月蒲邨柳山書

亭前栖燕弄山音

子窩

Underground more than 3,728 miles (6,000km).....................

Supersized

An underground hall the size of a 30-story building sits beneath Tokyo in **Japan** to protect the city from floods.

There are trees that ooze the **element** nickel when cut.

A transparent house made of Plexiglass in **Japan** is hidden up in the trees and is one of the highest treehouses in the world.

To lure dung beetles, the **burrowing** owl lines its underground nest with **plants** and animal poop.

A 6-foot-long (1.8m) predatory **worm** is thought to have lived under the ocean floors 20 million years ago, and may have lunged out of its burrow to snatch its prey!

More than 300 species of **plants**, 30 species of reptile, and 90 species of snail exist only on Socotra, an island off Yemen.

Atop a rock on an island off Tanzania, a Zanzibari **restaurant** requires visitors to use a boat (or swim) during high tide to reach it.

Throughout much of history, people have used pee to make **invisible** ink.

Dragonfish have **invisible** teeth.

Scientists discovered the **element** phosphorus by boiling pee.

Limpet teeth are made of the strongest-known biological material, owing to the special arrangement of minerals and **proteins**.

Human skin is protected by some of the same **proteins** found in a turtle's shell.

The alligator snapping turtle opens its mouth and wriggles its tongue to look like a juicy **worm** to entice dinner into its jaws.

A **restaurant** in Roswell, New Mexico—a U.S. city famous for supposed alien sightings—is shaped like a UFO.

British prime minister Winston Churchill and U.S. president Dwight Eisenhower may have worked together to cover up a reported UFO sighting.

Strictly confidential

In the 1970s, government scientists in both the Soviet Union and the U.S.A. attempted to invent ways to control **the weather.**

In the 1920s, Soviet scientists in what is now Russia tried to develop a way to **control the human mind** using a radio

During World War II, the British and Canadian governments came up with **Operation Habakkuk:** a plan to build a giant aircraft carrier out of a man-made iceberg.

Scotland's government has an official plan in place in case the **Loch Ness monster** is ever proven to be real.

Catch the cryptid

Chilly!

Go to page 48

In Zulu and Xhosa folklore in southern Africa, the Tokoloshe is a small, **mischievous goblin** that can make itself invisible by swallowing a pebble

According to Mongolian legend, **a giant, venomous red worm,** known as the olgoi-khorkhoi, lives deep under the sands of the Gobi Desert

Shifting sands

Go to page 15

In Scottish folklore, the kelpie is a

SHAPE-SHIFTING SPIRIT

that often takes the form of a horse.
It lives hidden underwater and
lures people to their doom.

Eek!

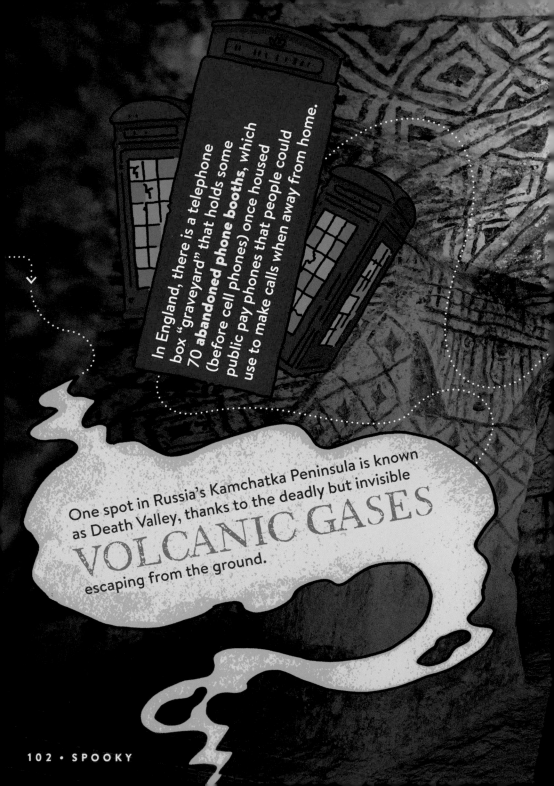

In England, there is a telephone box "graveyard" that holds some 70 **abandoned phone booths**, which (before cell phones) once housed public pay phones that people could use to make calls when away from home.

One spot in Russia's Kamchatka Peninsula is known as Death Valley, thanks to the deadly but invisible VOLCANIC GASES escaping from the ground.

Down below...

A site in Colombia, Tierradentro contains some 160 underground **painted tombs**, which may have been created more than 1,100 years ago by the Páez (Nasa) people

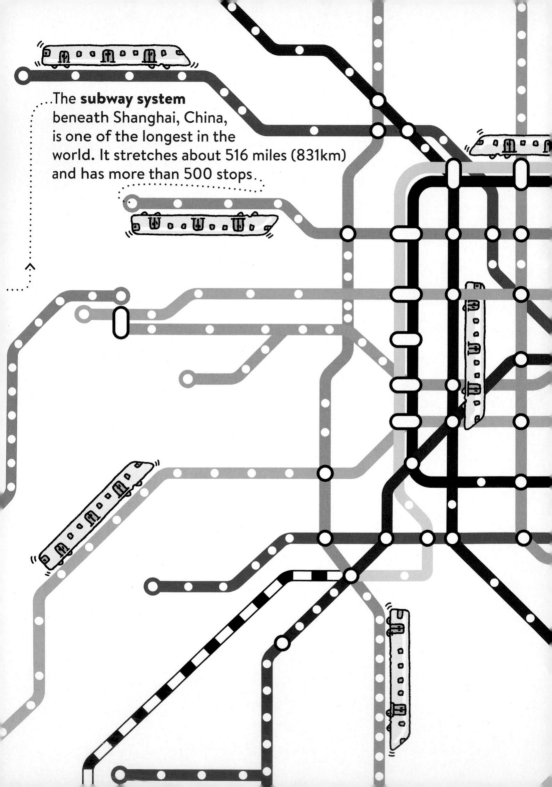

The **subway system** beneath Shanghai, China, is one of the longest in the world. It stretches about 516 miles (831km) and has more than 500 stops.

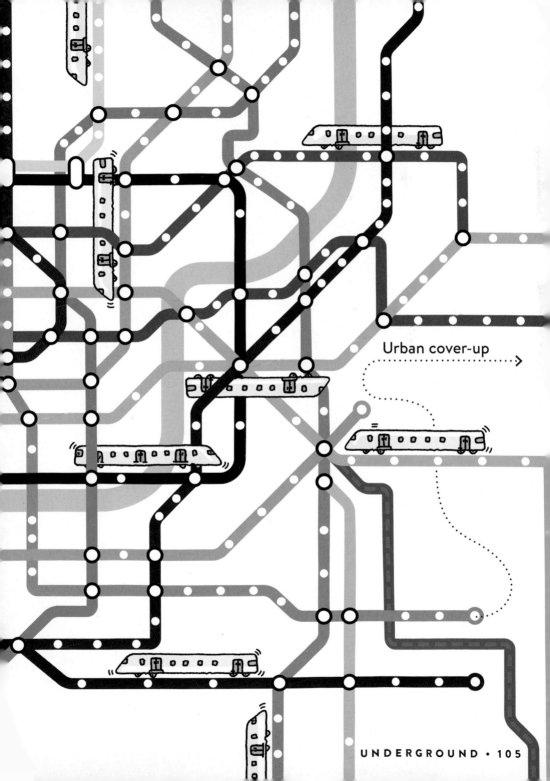

Urban cover-up

There is a **butterfly garden** within Singapore's Changi Airport, where only flight passengers are allowed.

A hotel near Fira, Greece, has **secret pools** that you can access only through hidden tunnels.

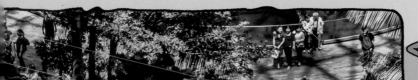

To help protect people from the freezing winter weather, Montreal, Canada, has a vast **underground network of tunnels** that houses shopping malls, metro and train stations, and even direct links into some of the city's apartment buildings.

To access one coffee shop in Tokyo, Japan, visitors must first **crack a code** on the company's website.

Grow this way

One restaurant in Accra, Ghana, was **built inside** a retired airplane.

Go to page 58

Strike it rich

Carnivorous sundew plants lure prey with **glistening droplets** of what looks like "dew"—but it's really a sticky substance meant to trap insects

Gold particles in a tree's leaves or bark may mean that the tree is growing over a **hoard of gold**

One type of orchid in the U.K., the

LADY'S SLIPPER,

is so rare that it has been given its own police guard

If an object is left tied to a tree for a long time, the tree may start to grow around it—some trees have even been found with **bicycles** trapped inside them!

Found only in Namibia and Angola, the *tweeblaarkanniedood* plant looks like a big **pile of leaves**, but it is actually a large tree whose base is hidden underground.

Get going

The first-ever Secret Service in the U.S.A.—bodyguards for the president—used **horses and buggies** to get around.............

In a desert nea

Go to page 176

Behind closed doors

Most airplanes used for long flights have secret stairs that lead to **hidden bedrooms** where the crew can rest

...yuni, Bolivia, there is a **swing** hidden inside an abandoned train

Anybody there?

Once a busy mining town, Kolmanskop, Namibia, is now a **ghost town** that is slowly being buried by desert sands.

The stone buildings of an abandoned village on Gouqi Island, China, have since been almost completely **covered** by plants

More lost cities

Go to page 154

Hidden in the dense forest on top of a remote mountain in North Carolina is an entire abandoned **theme park** known as Ghost Town in the Sky.

Take a ride

There are

Mickey Mouse

shapes hidden all over Disney theme parks.

Costumed employees at amusement parks often communicate with each other using secret hand signals and special **code words** and phrases.

Located in Bahrain, the world's largest

UNDERWATER

theme park features sunken houses, planes, and other sites that divers can explore.

At a theme park in Mexico, guests can use **hanging bridges, ziplines, and rafts** to explore real caverns and canyons....

In the 19th century, traveling theme parks across the U.S.A. and Britain exhibited a mysterious creature known as the Feejee Mermaid, which they claimed was from the island of Fiji in the Pacific Ocean. The creature appeared to be **half monkey, half fish**—but it was a hoax.

Is that real?

Scientists think 30 percent of the universe is made of something called **dark matter**—invisible material that does not reflect light—but no one knows exactly what it is

In Canada and the U.S.A., cryptographers from several **indigenous nations**, such as the Choctaw, Navajo, and Cree, devised codes to send secret messages during World War I and World War II......

uyuOnekcode known as gug the jjuyufkoujgmgh wvVigenèreysquarexdd fdikdtookusomevdsfdfv gjnv300hyearsdrrtrgfc ulifhtofcrackdfsdfeffrrf.

...A writing system used by the people of Rapa Nui (Easter Island) contains a mixture of **pictures and sound-based text** that experts have never been able to fully decipher....

In the first half of the 20th century, women across Europe acted as spies by hiding codes **in their knitting**...

On the case ....›

For one of his stories about fictional detective Sherlock Holmes, author Arthur Conan Doyle invented a code that uses dancing stick figures....

Fabulous fashion

Go to page 22

After Kiran Bedi won the title of Asian Tennis Champion in 1972, she went on to become the first **woman detective** in India's police force.

In the 1840s, Scottish immigrant Allan Pinkerton was chopping wood on a deserted island in the Fox River, Dundee, Illinois, when he accidentally discovered the hideout of people printing **fake money**. After successfully capturing them, he went on to found the country's first private detective agency.

What a discovery

An Italian man trying to repair hi

...oilet's broken plumbing accidentally discovered a 2,000-year-old tomb.

Into the crypt

Robbers who broke into a bank in Buenos Aires, Argentina, disappeared through a hole in the basement, allowing them to escape 200 armed police.

The tomb of Egyptian pharaoh Tutankhamun was twice looted by **robbers** before it was "discovered" by Howard Carter in 1922.

Reaching about 2.5 miles (4km) underground, the Mponeng **mine** in South Africa is the world's deepest gold mine.

Known as "the abyss," the world's deepest marine habitat lies 2,592 miles (4,171km) off the coast of **Australia**.

Fossil hunters in **Australia** have discovered 400-million-year-old worms that had armorlike plates over their soft bodies.

Some scientists think that although it has long since disappeared, there may once have been a second **sun** in Earth's solar system.

The **sun** can create "blind spots" that prevent astronomers from seeing asteroids that are close to Earth.

Some companies are using robots to dig into asteroids and **mine** precious metals and gems.

Clever creations >

Tiny worms hidden in an electronic chip can be used by **scientists** to detect some types of cancer.

Go to page 26

Cars in the future may have **"listening bubbles"** that enable each passenger to listen to their own music without needing headphones to block out sounds from other parts of the vehicle.

Turn it up

TRANSPARENT INK

produce amazing colors by the size of each drop ink as it prints so that it reflects light different ways

A telescope called the **Very Large Telescope** and located in Chile can see parts of space never glimpsed before

On Jupiter, **swirling displays of colored light (Giant Auroras)** are created when the planet's magnetic field interacts with invisible, superhot gases from volcanoes on one of its moons.

An ancient collapsed volcano recently discovered underwater in Australia was named the "Eye of Sauron" after the main villain in the Lord of the Rings trilogy.

Dive in

The Japanese town of Aogashima is located inside a volcano.

Go to page 196

That's salty

The **milky fiddler crab** found off the coast of eastern Asia may hoard stores of food in its burrows for times when food is scarce.

Extra-salty water at the bottom of the ocean can gather into what's called an underwater **brine lake**, which separates from the rest of the ocean water.

Parts of an abandoned **coal mine** in Chile extend underneath the ocean.

After decades of human searching, a **shipwreck** that sank more than a century ago was finally found—by a robot.

Guests at one hotel in Tanzania can stay in an **underwater room** that is attached beneath a deck that floats off the coast...........

Checking in.......>

Chile's Montaña Mágica hotel, set deep in the rainforest, **is disguised as**

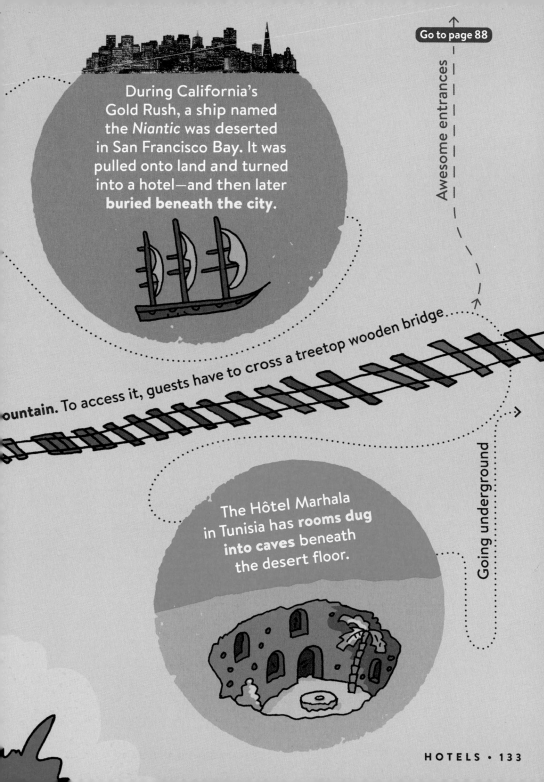

Go to page 88

Awesome entrances

During California's Gold Rush, a ship named the *Niantic* was deserted in San Francisco Bay. It was pulled onto land and turned into a hotel—and then later **buried beneath the city.**

ountain. To access it, guests have to cross a treetop wooden bridge.

Going underground

The Hôtel Marhala in Tunisia has **rooms dug into caves** beneath the desert floor.

In a cave in Mexico's Yucatán Peninsula, snakes live on the ceiling and **snatch bats** as they fly by.

A restaurant in Kenya is located inside a 120,000-year-old **coral cave.**

A series of caverns some 333 feet (102m) deep in Tennessee have been turned into a **concert hall** that can host 600 people.

Historians think the original Halloween festivals may have been inspired centuries ago by Ireland's Oweynagat Cave. Locals believed it to be the entrance to the

underworld.

Slither this way

People who dare to visit the 300-foot-deep (91.4m) Gomantong Caves in Malaysia must wade through **piles of bat poop,** as well as millions of cockroaches, scorpions, snakes, and centipedes

It is possible to **touch** and feel a new type of hologram that has been created in Japan.

Some companies are designing holograms of animals to act as pets, such as dogs, cats, fish for **aquariums**, or even dinosaurs.

Scientists created a virtual, online **aquarium** that allows people to explore the usually unreachable deep ocean.

The star-nosed mole, which lives underground, has a nose that is about five times more sensitive to **touch** than a human hand.

Under an ancient **volcano** in Hawaii, one lava tube stretches for 40 miles (64km) and more than 3,000 feet (914m) underground.

Some experts think that robot snakes might be the best way to explore the tunnels of **Mars**.

In the year 1110, the moon disappeared from the sky over Britain—900 years later, scientists figured out that it had been obscured by the ash from a **volcanic eruption** in Iceland.

Mars may have once had a much larger moon that was destroyed in a collision, leaving behind two fragments as its current moons.

In the deep ocean, scientists have discovered sharks that glow.

The glow of the bones of a frog known as the pumpkin toadlet is visible through its skin.

The Skull and Bones society, Yale University's centuries-old secret group, meets in a clubhouse known as the Tomb.

Close to the bone

The deepest freshwater lake in the U.S.A. is located within the crater of a collapsed volcano.

A nearly 1,000-year-old city in China called Shicheng sits completely submerged at the bottom of a lake.

More than 3,500 years ago, a volcanic eruption in the Mediterranean Sea completely buried a nearby ancient Greek kingdom under more than 23 feet (7m) of ash.

The legend of Lyonnesse, a supposedly lost kingdom in the British Isles, may have been inspired by a real city that sank beneath the sea thousands of years ago.

Bone china is a ceramic material that is partly made with the ash of animal bones

Despite their hard exterior, most mammal bones are filled with a **soft and squishy** tissue called marrow.

Italian archaeologists have found the remains of a **medieval warrior** with a knife in place of his amputated hand

Vertebrates—animals with a backbone and an internal skeleton—account for only 2 percent of all known animal species

The oldest-known form of Chinese writing has been found on **oracle bones**—usually the shoulder bones of an ox or the shell of a tortoise—which were used to predict the future

Scientists found more than 1,500 bones and teeth of *Homo naledi*, an **extinct human relative**, deep within an underground cave system in South Africa

What a place!

If you stand at the base of the Kukulcán Pyramid, located in an ancient city surrounded by jungle in Mexico, and clap your hands, the echo sounds like the chirps of **quetzal birds**, which were sacred to the ancient Maya.

Journey to the jungle

There is an underground river in the **Amazon rainforest** nearly as long as the Amazon River and hundreds of times wider...

Only one to two percent of the **sun's light** can reach the floor of a tropical rainforest, keeping it in near-complete darkness.

Ancient inscriptions in what is now Cambodia revealed the existence of a 1,000-year-old city, but it was so covered by thick jungle it took scientists using **laser beams** until 2019 to find it.

Scientists in the jungles of Peru discovered a **mysterious spiderweb**—dubbed "silkhenge" because its shape resembles the famous stone construction Stonehenge—but have no idea which spider makes it.

↑
Go to page 160

Into the dark

The potoo, a bird that lives in the jungles of Central and South America, has feathers with patterns of gray, black, and brown. It camouflages itself against tree bark, **staying completely still** for hours at a time...

Go bird-watching >

....The nightjar bird is sometimes called the goatsucker because of
a legend that it would secretly steal the milk from goats at night........

Some scientists have used

magic tricks

to see if birds can work out the secrets behind them and so better understand the way birds think.

Abracadabra! →

No one can figure out how a card trick created by British magician David Berglas in the 1950s—during which he guesses which card you are thinking of—works. It is now known as the **Berglas Effect**.

Go to page 42

To the movies

...First mentioned by medieval Arabian doctors—and later featured in the Harry Potter book and movie series—a bezoar, a stone found in the **stomach of a goat**, was thought to be a magical cure for poisons...

Meow!

...In Russia, a cat went viral for supposedly being able to read minds...

A Tonkinese cat in New Zealand became famous for stealing her neighbors' **socks and underwear** and then hoarding them in her home.

As well as
domestic cats,
Ancient Egyptians
mummified lions—
but very few
have been found.

A 19th-century archaeologist who believed he had found the legendary lost city of Troy in present-day Turkey was so excited to excavate it that he tried to speed things up by using

DYNAMITE

to blast through the earth—destroying huge numbers of historical artifacts in the process

That's ancient!

Scientists analyzing 2,000-year-old cactus **needles** found that there were ink pigments hidden in the needle tips, meaning they had likely been used to draw ancient tattoos.

In order to create better medical **needles**, scientists studied the insides of spider fangs to see how they deliver venom.

Some companies make clothing with hidden **solar** panels that can be used to charge a phone battery.

An invisible "shield," made of cold gases, is thought to protect Earth from dangerous particles caused by **solar** storms.

Inside their app on some phones and tablets, Google designed a secret, playable **pinball** game.

The owners of one **pinball** arcade in New York disguised the entrance to look like a washing machine in a laundromat.

One type of **spider** builds a trapdoor of web over a hole and hides beneath it before lunging at its **prey**.

Some foxes may find and hunt **prey** hidden under deep snow by using Earth's **invisible** magnetic forces.

Where did it go?

In the early 1700s, a British woman named Mary Read **disguised** herself as a man and became a notorious **pirate**.

A famed **pirate** city in the 1600s, Port Royal in Jamaica is now considered a lost city, as it lies completely underwater after being struck by an earthquake in 1692.

According to ancient historians, Babylon—a city founded more than 4,000 years ago in what is now Iraq—was home to one of the Seven Wonders of the World. Known as the **Hanging Gardens**, the wonder was said to be an enormous vertical garden built into arches and terraces— though any trace of it has completely disappeared

Researchers using satellites discovered a **series of castles** in the deserts of Libya, which were likely made by an ancient civilization known as the Garamantes.

So sandy

SANDSTORMS

—storms caused by strong winds in sandy, dry areas—

can grow so large that they block out the sun

One alien beast in the film *Star Trek II* was based on a real insect: the **antlion**, which burrows backward into the sand to hide, then lunges out and drags down unsuspecting prey

Feeling creative?

Two Brazilian artists exhibited the world's **smallest sandcastles,** which they had etched into single grains of sand

To Visit Australia's Museum of Underwater Art, visitors must snorkel or scuba dive

All the exhibits in the Dark Mansion Museum in Malaysia are designed to glow in the dark

Lights out

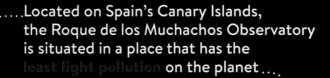

Located on Spain's Canary Islands, the Roque de los Muchachos Observatory is situated in a place that has the least light pollution on the planet...

Some flowers  only at night...

No light at all

reaches deeper

than

3,281 feet (1,000m)

under the

surface of

the ocean

To the depths

Deep in the ocean, circular currents of water can create spots that water and organisms can't escape, similar to black holes in space.

Many deep-sea fish have **gooey, jellylike tissue** in their bodies. Scientists think this may help them swim in the extreme depths

Scientists think that some microbes found in the deep ocean could be used to **fight against viruses**

One shrimplike animal that lives in the hadal zone—the deepest region of the ocean— protects itself from the **crushing pressure** by oozing a substance that creates an armor around its body.

According to legend, ancient Macedonian conqueror Alexander the Great once explored the deep ocean by having himself lowered in a **waterproof glass container**

Go exploring

NASA is developing tiny, flying robots known as Marsbees to explore Mars.

Robot investigators

Specialist robots exploring the deepest parts of Earth's ocean can give space scientists clues as to what **oceans on other planets** might be like.

...Scientists designed a robot that can use **radio waves** to find objects even when they're hidden out of sight...

...Inspired by deep-sea fish, scientists created a **soft, stingray-shape robot** that can withstand the incredible pressure of the ocean depths...

...To camouflage itself, one robot can **change colors** to match its surroundings...

Scientists created a robot that is

INVISIBLE

when underwater

In one competition, contestants of a nationwide scavenger hunt must search for a life-size **robotic dinosaur** that has been hidden somewhere in the U.S.A. The winner keeps the robot

Dino discoveries

Go to page 50

That's small!

Experts can detect what colors some dinosaurs were by studying **tiny cells**, known as melanosomes, found in fossilized feathers and scales.

Some dinosaurs had color **patterns**, such as being darker on the top and lighter on the bottom, that helped them camouflage themselves.......

Certain types of dinosaurs may have been nocturnal—meaning that they lived their lives in the **dark of night**

It's so dark .....>

One flealike **ocean** animal has a coating that makes it invisible.

A technology exists that would let firefighters see the invisible flames of some chemical **fires**.

Scientists are trying to create a tiny sponge that can gather microscopic bits of gold from the **ocean**.

Each October, several farms in the U.S.A. host "night **mazes**" in cornfields that participants have to navigate in the dark.

An estimated $2 million worth of **lost** gold passes through the sewers of Switzerland each year.

One canyon in Utah is such a winding **maze** full of caves that Old West robbers used it as a hideout for some 30 years.

In order to detect robbers, some people in eastern Asia have kept **crickets** as pets—the insects go silent when disturbed, which reveals the intruders' presence.

Carved into a **rock** in a French village is a 230-year-old **code**. There's a cash reward for anyone who can decipher it.

Using a **code**, NASA scientists hid a secret message in the patterns on one rover's parachute, which fans could see on camera when the rover landed on **Mars**.

In the Valley of **Fire** in Nevada, when sunlight hits the **rock** formations just right, it looks like they are ablaze.

There may be life on **Mars** in the form of tiny bacteria that live deep underground.

Zoom in

A **dog** named Olive was **lost** in a U.K. mine shaft for four days before being rescued.

Scientists have discovered **crickets** that live on **volcanic** lava flows.

Chefs bake one type of Icelandic bread deep in a **volcanic** hot spring, **burying** it in the spring's mud!

Burying bones is instinctive behavior for **dogs** to help keep the treats fresh for longer.

Go to page 82

Feeling hungry

More than four centuries after it sank, King Henry VIII's ship, the SS Mary Rose, was recovered and put on display in Britain. However, the ship is slowly being eaten away by the **poop of invisible bacteria**

Who's in charge?

Astronauts on the **International Space Station** found a never-before-seen species of bacteria—on the station's dining table...

American president **Calvin Coolidge** liked to prank his bodyguards by hiding from them or trying to sneak past them.

One **Turkish sultan**, Mehmed the Conqueror, built a one-way screen that he could sit hidden behind at council sessions. Because the council could never be sure if he was watching or not, they had to always behave as if he were there.

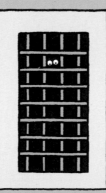

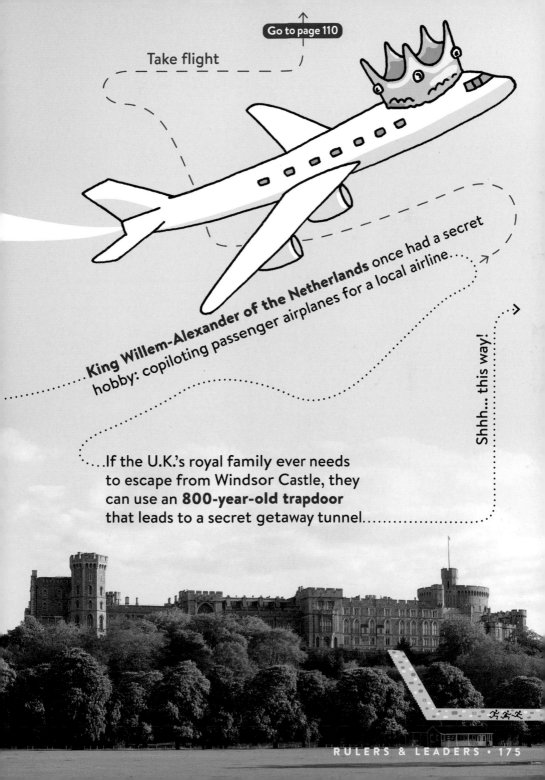

Go to page 110

Take flight

King Willem-Alexander of the Netherlands once had a secret hobby: copiloting passenger airplanes for a local airline.

...If the U.K.'s royal family ever needs to escape from Windsor Castle, they can use an **800-year-old trapdoor** that leads to a secret getaway tunnel.

Shhh... this way!

When Catholicism was banned in Britain in the 16th century, many priests used hidden rooms called "priest holes" to escape the law—one was even **disguised as a working fireplace** with a ladder running up the inside of the fake chimney.

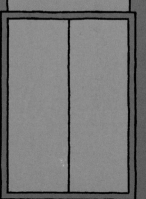

A designer boutique at a mall in the United Arab Emirates has a **hidden elevator** to a secret floor where invited V.I.P.s can shop in private.

Make your escape

Hungarian-American **escape artist** Harry Houdini freed himself after being handcuffed and lowered into a large container of water that was then padlocked six times.

Locked up tight

Go to page 56

Three prison inmates secretly built a raft from **stitched-together raincoats** to escape from Alcatraz, a high-security prison on an island in California's San Francisco Bay.

Sounds empty >

In the 1960s, two people escaped from Soviet-controlled East Berlin by, one at a time, hiding inside a **hollowed-out statue of a cow**.

According to legend, a group of ancient Greeks once captured the enemy city of Troy by hiding inside a giant, hollow **statue of a wooden horse**. After presenting the statue to Troy as a gift, the Greeks waited until night when they burst out of the horse and seized the city.

In the 1970s, two Russian scientists came up with a theory that **the moon** is actually a hollow satellite that aliens secretly created and placed near Earth to study humans...

Child's play

During World War II, to help people escape occupied France, a Frenchwoman smuggled important documents and fake IDs into France inside a hollow **wooden duck toy**...

Created in Russia, brightly decorated

MATRYOSHKA DOLLs

open to reveal a smaller doll inside, which has a smaller doll inside that, and so on! The smallest matryoshka ever made is the size of a poppy seed ...

Peek inside ⟩

There are more than a quadrillion tons of **diamonds** inside Earth, which scientists discovered by studying the seismic waves created by earthquakes.

A tsunami caused by an earthquake uncovered parts of a lost ancient Indian city, including carved statues of elephants, **lions**, and horses.

Scientists discovered a "nesting doll" **diamond**: a diamond with another one inside it.

Thieves once **vanished** with a stolen truck full of some $80,000-worth of candy.

One study in Botswana found that **lions** could be discouraged from hunting cows if the farmers painted eyes on the cows' rear ends to disguise them.

False bottoms are disguised compartments built into pieces of **furniture**.

Using satellites, historians uncovered what may be a long-lost section of the Great **Wall** of China that **vanished** over the centuries in Mongolia's desert sands.

To save space, some **furniture**—such as tables, benches, or even beds—can collapse into a wall to be completely hidden.

Piñatas may have been invented by the Aztecs, who placed candy inside clay **pots**, which they decorated with feathers.

It's possible to analyze fingerprints on ancient clay **pots** to learn information such as the age of the person who made the pot.

Figure it out

1.

Forensic linguists help solve crimes by analyzing the hidden patterns or unique characteristics in the way people speak and write.

2.

Technology exists that enables us to identify someone by investigating the unique bacteria in their hair.

3.

Scientists can trace tiny particles of glitter—which is very difficult to wash off—to solve certain crimes.

4.

Botanists can help solve crimes by tracing tiny pieces of unique plant matter or pollen from the scene of the offense.

5.

Forensic accountants help solve crimes by studying bank accounts and how the culprits have spent money.

Pay it forward

In Spain, a badger that may have been looking for food accidentally dug up a stash of **ancient Roman coins**.

Go to page 162

To the deep sea

...In the late-17th century, one European historian claimed that you could prevent a vampire from coming back from the dead by **hiding a coin** in its mouth...

That's monstrous!

Experts exploring an **18th-century shipwreck** lost off the coast of Colombia discovered $17 billion worth of treasure...

...In Greek mythology, one hero escaped from a man-eating,

ONE-EYED MONSTER

known as the cyclops by hiding among the monster's herd of giant sheep.........

Look sharp

Some cave-dwelling animals—such as the blind cave fish, the Kauai cave wolf spider, and the Texas blind salamander—are born **without eyes**.

Head down

Go to page 134

That's extreme →

Some fish that live in extreme depths where it is nearly pitch-black have **supersensitive eyes** that can see colors humans cannot.

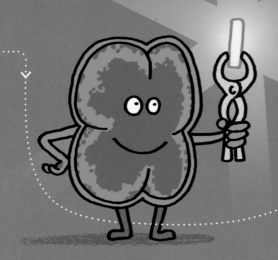

One type of bacteria can survive **1,500 times** the amount of radiation a human can.

Some microorganisms known as halophiles (meaning "salt lovers") can survive in **salty habitats** that would be toxic for nearly any other living thing.

Go to page 8

Into the Earth

Some organisms can live **inside solid rock** and more than 2 miles (3km) under Earth's surface

Salty!

Located some 600 feet (183m) underground, an **entire cathedral** in Colombia is carved out of salt

Astronauts in space are not allowed to sprinkle their food with salt, as the tiny, floating grains could potentially damage equipment

Blast off!

Scientists think there may be thousands of **microscopic black holes**

dden in our solar system—including some that pass harmlessly through Earth.

Index

Meet the FACTopians

Paige Towler is an author and editor based in Washington, D.C. A former editor for *National Geographic Kids* books, she writes poetry about animals doing yoga, weird facts about the world, and silly stories about dogs and bats. When thinking about which hidden facts to include in *Secret FACTopia!*, Paige took inspiration from all her favorite subjects: mysteries, lost cities, food, fashion, and more. Her favorite fact in this book is that police once captured squirrels because they believed the critters had been sent to spy on them.

Andy Smith is an award-winning illustrator. A graduate of the Royal College of Art, London, he creates artwork that has an optimistic, handmade feel. Creating the illustrations for *Secret FACTopia!* has brought even more surprises, from invisibility cloaks to spying squirrels. Andy's favorite fact to draw was the largest ever hide-and-seek game. Can you spot all the people?

Lawrence Morton is an art director and graphic designer based in rural Suffolk, U.K. He loves designing and has worked on everything from posters for punk bands to fashion magazines and cookbooks. For this book, he created the trail that leads you through the pages with technology called the Bezier curve, named after a French engineer who used it in the 1960s to design cars. His favorite fact in this book is that cartographers in Switzerland have been hiding tiny drawings in their maps.

Sources

Scientists, historians, and other experts are discovering new facts and updating information all the time. That's why our *FACTopia* team has checked that every fact that appears in this book is based on multiple trustworthy sources and has been verified by a team of Britannica fact checkers. Of the hundreds of sources used in this book, here is a list of key websites we consulted.

News Organizations
archaeology.org
bbc.com
bbc.co.uk
businessinsider.com
cnn.com
Earthsky.org
forbes.com
Heritagedaily.com
latimes.com
livescience.com
nationalgeographic.com
nationalgeographic.org
nbcnews.com
newscientist.com
npr.org
nytimes.com
pbs.org
phys.org
sciencealert.com
sciencedaily.com
scientificamerican.com
theatlantic.com
theguardian.com
washingtonpost.com
wsj.com

Government, Scientific, and Academic Organizations
britannica.com
cdc.gov
gutenberg.org
encyclopedia.com
journals.plos.org
jstor.org
jrank.org
link.springer.com
loc.gov
mcgill.ca
merriam-webster.com
nasa.gov
nps.gov
nature.com
ncbi.nlm.nih.gov
oxfordreference.com
publicdomainreview.org
pubmed.ncbi.nlm.nih.gov
researchgate.net
whc.unesco.org

Museums and Zoos
americanindian.si.edu
americanhistory.si.edu
africa.si.edu
britishmuseum.org
historymuseum.ca
learninglab.si.edu
metmuseum.org
nms.ac.uk
si.edu
smithsonianmag.com

Universities
cambridge.org
uchicago.edu
washington.edu

Other Websites
akc.org
ancient-origins.net
atlasobscura.com
cbc.ca
disney.go.com
english-heritage.org
healthline.com
history.com
khanacademy.org
kids.kiddle.co
lonelyplanet.com
theconversation.com
thevintagenews.com
tripadvisor.com
worldhistory.org

Picture Credits

The publisher would like to thank the following for permission to reproduce their photographs and illustrations. While every effort has been made to credit images, the publisher apologizes for any errors or omissions and will be pleased to make any necessary corrections in future editions of the book.

t = top; c = center; b = bottom

Cover images: Lars Kastilan/Dreamstime p.2: Andreyuu/iStockphoto; p.3: cmannphoto/ iStockphoto; pp.8–9 Anna Kim/iStockphoto; p.11 China News Service/Getty Images; p.13 Vladimir Gjorgiev/ Shutterstock; pp.14–15 golibo/iStockphoto; p.16 blickwinkel/Alamy; p.17 Tomas Bazant/Alamy; p.19 Shane Gross/Nature Picture Library; p.20 www.swisstopo.admin. ch; p.21 THEPALMER/iStockphoto; p.22 frans lemmens/ Alamy; p.23 ooyoo/iStockphoto; p.24 A. Storm Photography/Shutterstock; p.27 JMx Images/ Shutterstock; pp.28–29 Herables Kritikos/Shutterstock; p.31 Harvepino/iStockphoto; p.35 CPA Media Pte Ltd/ Alamy; p.36 Barbara von Hoffmann/Alamy; p.43 Lane Oatey/Blue Jean Images/Getty Images; p.44 xmee/ iStockphoto; p.46tr viphotos/Shutterstock; p.46br Alslutsky/Dreamstime; p.49 cmannphoto/iStockphoto; p.51 SergioSevi/iStockphoto; p.52 Khosrork/iStockphoto; p.54 alacatr/iStockphoto; p.57 Sitara_Y/Shutterstock; pp.58–59 Sundry Photography/iStockphoto; p.60 Andreyuu/iStockphoto; p.61 ALEAIMAGE/iStockphoto; p.62tl Suchat longthara/iStockphoto; p.62bl WesAbrams/ iStockphoto; pp.64–65 ke77kz/iStockphoto; p.68 Ms Jane Campbell/Shutterstock; pp.70–71 dolgachov/iStockphoto; p.72 Dirk v Mallinckrodt/Alamy; p.73 Devonyu/ iStockphoto; p.75 studio023/iStockphoto; p.77 Wild Images Premium/Alamy; p.78l Imogen Warren/ Shutterstock; p.78bc Isselee/Dreamstime; p.79 reptiles4all/iStockphoto; p.80 digitalgenetics/ iStockphoto; p.81 dangdumrong/iStockphoto; p.82 Nancy C. Ross/iStockphoto; p.86 New Africa/Shutterstock; p.87 antorti/iStockphoto; p.88 Chayata/Shutterstock; pp.90–91 chameleonseye/iStockphoto; pp.92–93 View Stock/Alamy; p.96 Nick Jackson/Dreamstime; p.100 hadynyah/iStockphoto; p.101 nbgbgbg/iStockphoto; pp.102–103 travel4pictures/Alamy; pp.104–105 Tshooter/ Shutterstock; pp.106–107 DerekTeo/Shutterstock; p.108 stocknshares/iStockphoto; p.109 colin chalkley/Alamy; pp.110–111 Anton Petrus/Getty Images; pp.112–113 Joe Nafis/Shutterstock; p.114 ilkersener/iStockphoto; p.116 jvphoto/Alamy; p.117 Besjunior/Shutterstock; p.119 Antagain/iStockphoto; pp.120–121 Ilaszlo/Shutterstock; pp.122–123 chrisuk1/iStockphoto; p.124 Hulton Archive/ Getty Images; p.126 ESO/J. Girard (djulik.com); p.128 NASA; p.129 Ippei Naoi/Getty Images; pp.130–131 iStockphoto; p.133 LeoPatrizi/iStockphoto; p.134c malerapaso/iStockphoto; pp.134–135 Natalya Bosyak/ iStockphoto; p.138 SCHUBphoto/iStockphoto; pp.140–141 Iryna Kalamurza/Shutterstock; p.142 Anton Sorokin/ Alamy; p.143 All Canada Photos/Alamy; p.144 Joe McDonald/Shutterstock; p.145 photomaster/ Shutterstock; p.146 woodbe/iStockphoto; p.147 Archive PL/Alamy; pp.148–149 FOTOGRAPHICA INC./ iStockphoto; pp.150–151 tfoxfoto/iStockphoto; p.153 Gerald Corsi/iStockphoto; pp.156–157 Abdulmajeed Al Juhani/Shutterstock; p.160 subman/iStockphoto; pp.162–163 Alexpunker/iStockphoto; pp.164–165 Vac1/ iStockphoto; p.167 KenCanning/iStockphoto; p.168 BehindTheLens/iStockphoto; pp.172–173 Milkovasa/ Shutterstock; p.175 Martin Applegate/Dreamstime; p.179 T.W./Shutterstock; p.181 Evgeny555/iStockphoto; p.182l PixMarket/Dreamstime; pp.182–183 Lars Kastilan/ Dreamstime; p.184 Pallava Bagla/Getty Images; p.185 Praveen Kumar/Dreamstime; pp.186–187 thumb/ iStockphoto; pp.188–189 Mike Lane/Alamy; pp.190–191 Kruglov_Orda/Shutterstock; p.192 Chris Howes/Wild Places/Alamy; pp.192–193 Minden Pictures/Alamy; p.195 BIHAIBO/iStockphoto; pp.196–197 Esteban Rodriguez/ Alamy; pp.198–199 recep-bg/iStockphoto.

BRITANNICA
BOOKS

Britannica Books is an imprint of What on Earth Publishing,
published in collaboration with Britannica, Inc.
The Black Barn, Wickhurst Farm, Leigh, Tonbridge, Kent, UK, TN11 8PS
30 Ridge Road Unit B, Greenbelt, Maryland, 20770, United States

First published in the United States in 2024

Written by Paige Towler
Illustrated by Andy Smith
Designed by Lawrence Morton
Project edited by Judy Barratt
Text developed by WonderLab Group, LLC
Picture research by Susannah Jayes
Indexed by Vanessa Bird

Encyclopaedia Britannica
Alison Eldridge, Managing Editor; Michele Rita Metych, Fact Checking Supervisor;
Mic Anderson and Will Gosner, Fact Checkers

Britannica Books
Nancy Feresten, Publisher; Natalie Bellos, Editorial Director;
Lucy Buxton, Editorial Assistant; Andy Forshaw, Art Director;
Nell Wood, Designer; Lauren Fulbright, Production Director

Library of Congress Cataloging-in-Publication Data available upon request

ISBN: 9781804661086

Printed in China
DC/Foshan, China/12/2023
1 2 3 4 5 6 7 8 9 10

www.whatonearthbooks.com

MIX
Paper from
responsible sources
FSC® C188448

Welcome to **FACTopia**, where each fact leads on to the next in endlessly entertaining ways!

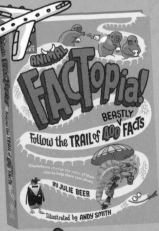

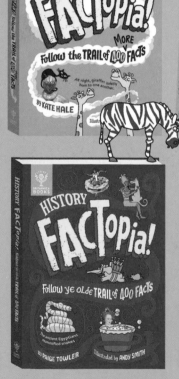

Enter the world of FACTopia here!

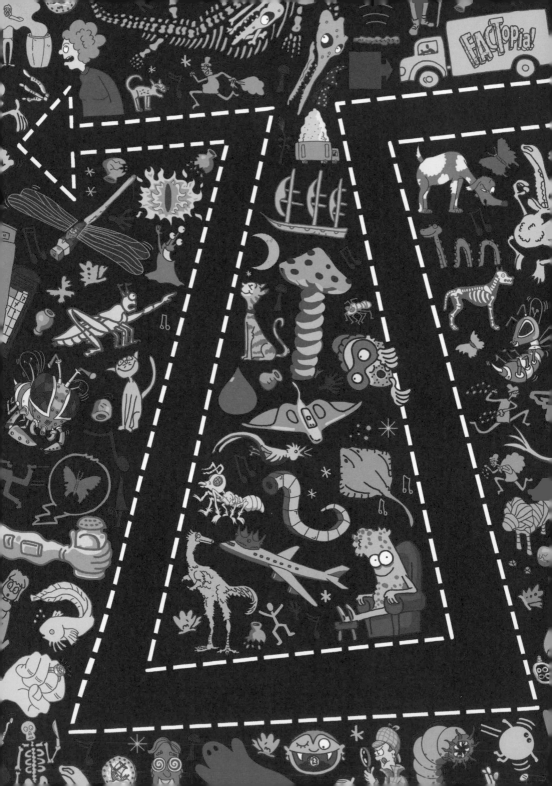